# WELSH POTTERY

by

## Robert Pugh

## A TOWY GUIDE

*The Potteries of South Wales*

THE CAMBRIAN POTTERY, SWANSEA (1764-1870)

THE GLAMORGAN POTTERY, SWANSEA (1813-1839)

THE SOUTH WALES POTTERY, LLANELLY (1839-1922)

# Acknowledgements

FOR ALL OF US WRITING ABOUT, or taking an interest in, Welsh ceramics, our main source of help and inspiration is, and one imagines always will be, the late Morton Nance. His monumental work 'The Pottery and Porcelain of Swansea and Nantgarw' is arguably the finest book on any ceramic factory or area, and we must consider ourselves fortunate that it was to Welsh ceramics that Nance devoted his life.

I should also like to acknowledge the help given to me in the writing of this small book, by my co-author of 'Llanelly Pottery', Gareth Hughes, and also Rowland Williams and Roderick Evans. They are jointly responsible for any scholarship it may contain. Thanks too to Clive Reed who gave me useful help on Ynysmeudwy Pottery.

I take this opportunity to acknowledge a debt to two people who helped me form an early interest in Welsh ceramics – Dilys Jenkins, who taught me that Llanelly Pottery was the most interesting pottery in the world, and Richie Maddock, who showed me that Dilys might not have been entirely correct.

I should particularly like to thank Peter Douglas-Jones for taking the majority of the photographs and Sotheby's for supplying those from the Sir Leslie Joseph Collection. Thanks, too, to my wife Carol for proof-reading.

Many items photographed are from private collections and I would like to thank those collectors for their help. The remaining items are from Robert Pugh Antiques.

We have based our illustrations of marks on those used in the 1914 Glyn-Vivian catalogue and 'Swansea Blue and White Pottery', by Stan Williams and Peter Pryce.

Published by
Towy Publishing, 2 Beaufort Mews, St. Saviour's Road, Larkhall, Bath BA1 6QF.

*Front cover:*
A Cambrian Pottery creamware botanical dish decorated with a *DWARF IRIS* by Thomas Pardoe, c.1800.

*Back cover:*
A Llanelly Pottery child's plate, with moulded alphabet border,
decorated with a cockerel, probably by Sarah Roberts, c.1910.

# Contents

*The Cambrian Pottery Swansea, engraved by Thomas Rothwell and published by Coles and Haynes in 1791.*

# The Cambrian Pottery
## 1764-1870

### THE EARLY YEARS (1764-1817)

ON JULY 31ST 1764 the Burgesses of Swansea (the body acting as the local authority of the time) granted to William Coles of Cadoxton, Neath, a lease of what had formerly been the copper works on the Strand at Swansea. So began that enterprise which was to last for more than a hundred years and was to attract so much of our attention for a hundred years more.

William Coles had set up the Pottery as an addition to his other extensive businesses and we have no reason to believe that he had any previous experience of the pottery industry. The Burgesses were keen to let the old copper-works site for a venture that was in keeping with their proposed image of Swansea, as a resort and bathing place. This was reflected in Coles' rent, and the Burgesses were successful in their aims, the pottery becoming an important 'upper class' tourist attraction. However, within fifteen years of the inception of the Pottery, certainly by 1779, William Coles had died. He left his considerable business interests to his three sons, Rowland Pytt, Edward and John. The eldest appears to have taken very little further interest in the Pottery and indeed it was unsuccessfully offered for sale in 1783.

It was Coles' youngest son, John, who in February of 1790 entered into a partnership with George Haynes, who was then manager and the most important influence in the early life of the Pottery. This new partnership obtained an extension to the lease and spent considerable capital on improvements. During the next ten years, Haynes brought the best talent he could find to Swansea and the factory (then for the first time known as the Cambrian Pottery) could compete on equal terms with Wedgwood.

In 1800, John Coles died. The Pottery continued production, managed solely by Haynes, to whom the lease was assigned, but the Coles family did retain a financial interest.

### THE ARRIVAL OF THE DILLWYNS

In 1777, William Dillwyn, a Quaker gentleman of Welsh descent, but born in the United States, made his second trip to Britain, travelling via Cork and Swansea. During his brief visit to Swansea he had visited the Pottery. Very soon afterwards, he married Sarah Weston, of Essex, and by the end of 1778 their son Lewis Weston Dillwyn was born.

In 1801, William visited Swansea again and, although he was never to call it home, he nonetheless took a great interest in the town. Subsequently, in 1802, he purchased

*Cambrian Elephant
pattern, c.1820.*

the lease to the Pottery from Haynes and the lease to the Pottery mill from the Duke of Beaufort. The actual business of the Pottery was bought on behalf of his son, who was to have seven-tenths of the profits, while Haynes retained three-tenths. This partnership then rented the premises from William Dillwyn. Lewis Weston Dillwyn was 24-years-old and a complete novice. George Haynes was 57 and already had some fifteen years' experience in the pottery. The business was then to be known as Haynes, Dillwyn and Co.

During the next seven years, the duration of the agreement between Dillwyn and Haynes, it would seem that the status quo was largely maintained and that the relationship worked despite young Dillwyn's preoccupation with his marriage and his scientific studies. At the end of that period, it was agreed that the arrangement should continue for another nine months but that Haynes should retire in March, 1810. During these eight years, the production of the pottery went on much as before.

At some stage, there seems to have been a disagreement, and although it appears that Haynes would have liked to have continued at the pottery, he had plenty of other strings to his bow. However, his assistant at the pottery was his son-in-law William Baker, who was not in this happy position and would have been without employment if Haynes had parted company from Dillwyn. This appears to have been a point of contention, and the actual departure of Haynes from the pottery seems to have been less friendly than it might have been. However, even looking back over 180 years, it can be seen that the difference in age, experience and background of the two men might easily have made their relationship difficult.

*Swansea (Cambrian)*
*Ladies with Baskets*
*pattern. Black transfer,*
*1824-30.*

In any event, Haynes went against the spirit of his partnership agreement and set out to antagonise Dillwyn by starting a soapworks on the site next to the Pottery under the guise of a new partnership. The result was that Dillwyn was forced to sue Haynes for this nuisance and won his case. Damages were minimal, just £10, but the Haynes partnership's expenses were some £1200.

This proved to be just the beginning of the quarrel between Dillwyn and Haynes, for immediately afterwards the firm of Baker, Bevan and Irwin was formed to set up a rival Pottery, the Glamorgan, on another site nearby. Haynes himself had no legal connection with the new firm but was, of course, influential through Baker, his son-in-law.

Following the retirement from the Pottery of George Haynes, Dillwyn decided, in 1811, to take into partnership Timothy Bevington (who had been promoted to pottery manager in 1810 and had previously been the confidential clerk), and his son, John Bevington. They were to receive seven-twentieths of the profits between them. Like Dillwyn, they were Quakers. For the next six years, the company was to be called Dillwyn and Co., and the pots marked accordingly.

In 1817, Lewis Weston Dillwyn's father-in-law, John Llewellyn, died, and Dillwyn decided to retire from the business of the Pottery to undertake the running of the Llewellyn estate at Penllergaer, some six miles from Swansea. Dillwyn's elder son, John, was John Llewellyn's heir and was a minor at the time. He later changed his name to Llewelyn and became well-known as a pioneer photographer and friend of Fox Talbot.

# THE DILLWYN FAMILY

WILLIAM DILLWYN
*London Quaker emigrated to America*

JOHN DILLWYN

WILLIAM DILLWYN
*Married Sarah Weston in London on moving from
America to Britain
Purchased Cambrian Pottery for:*

LEWIS WESTON DILLWYN
*Married Mary Adams
(natural daughter and heir of Col. John Llewelyn of Penllegaer)
Owned Pottery*

JOHN DILLWYN LLEWELYN (PHOTOGRAPHER)
*Changed name on inheriting
maternal grandfather's estate*

LEWIS LLEWELYN DILLWYN
*Married Elizabeth De La Beche
Owned Pottery*

MARY DE LA BECHE DILLWYN
*married John Cole Nichol
of Merthyr Mawr*

AMY DILLWYN

RICE MANSEL NICHOL
*assumed surname Dillwyn in 1904 as heir to his aunt, Amy Dillwyn*

The very first items to be produced at William Coles' factory were very utilitarian and are now generally unidentifiable, if they have survived at all. However, there were some items inscribed by a decoration scratched into the pots in blue cobalt and given a clear glaze. These items of 'scratch blue' are very rare. Inkpots, tea caddies and jugs are recorded but the earliest piece yet found is a small spirit-flask inscribed *'MORGAN JOHN SWANSEA MARCH Ye 28Th 1768.'*

These items are often described as being 'salt-glazed', a technique whereby salt is thrown into the kiln and fuses with the clay to form a glaze. Whilst salt-glaze was in common use in Staffordshire during the first half of the 18th century, by the time it arrived in Swansea it was somewhat old-fashioned. Morton Nance, in his monumental work on this subject, believed that this technique was not actually used at Swansea. The reasons for a possible confusion here are twofold. Firstly, traditional English salt-glaze pottery is often found decorated in scratch blue and thus there is a tendency to associate the two techniques; secondly, a salt-glaze finish has a slightly 'orange peel' feel to it, but Nance attributes this effect on Swansea products to the slight rough-ness of the surface of the pot under the glaze. We now tend to believe that salt-glaze *was* a technique used in Swansea, as well as ordinary clear glazes, and this would appear to be born out by an inscribed punch-bowl recently acquired by the Glyn-Vivian Art Gallery, and therefore not known to Nance.

Eventually, the early bodies gave way to the first examples of the creamware for which the Cambrian Pottery was to become so rightly famous. By the 1760s, Wedg-wood was already producing what he called Queen's Ware and Swansea was not going to be far behind. In 1777, when William Dillwyn first visited the Pottery, creamware was well in production and, indeed, is referred to in his journal as 'Queen's Ware'.

Throughout this early period, that is post-1783, the main production of the pottery was 'flat' ware for table use. This would have been bought by the wealthier classes, and was simply beyond the reach of most people, the quality of even the most commonly produced patterns, such as Long Bridge, being very high. Large supper-sets and huge dinner-services were the norm. Many items which were essentially functional were clearly made for purely decorative purposes, particularly jugs which were the objects usually chosen for elaborate decoration or inscription. Perhaps the best-known example of this are the wonderful, but sadly very rare, 'Cambrian' tiger jugs.

The Welsh factories generally produced very few purely ornamental items in the way that Staffordshire figures were produced. However, in this early period at the end of the eighteenth century and the early years of the nineteenth, an attempt was made at the Cambrian Pottery to introduce figures like those of Anthony and Cleopatra in yellow glaze or black basalt. These are now found in such small numbers, and by their very nature were less likely to be broken or damaged, that we must assume that they were produced only in experimental quantities. This also applies to the elabo-rate Egyptian-influenced candle-holders and to the classical 'Roman' lamps. These items were modelled by GEORGE BENTLEY, who was also responsible for large cane-ware vases and game-pie dishes, and the factory was never to achieve quite this quality of production or design again.

A small number of cherub figures were produced during this early period. Similar

*Swansea Pottery Jug inscribed 'Thomas Furness Wooden 1788'. (8").*

*[Note: Wooden is a village in Pembrokeshire. This is an important, early documentary jug].*

*The mark on the Jug in Plate 1.*

*Swansea creamware tea cannister inscribed in 'scratch blue', Elizabeth Bowen 1778, and a creamware tea caddy simplistically decorated in enamel colours. The silver lid is hallmarked for 1795 and engraved to match the decoration on the pottery.*

*Top left: Vase base on dolphin supports decorated in cobalt blue.*
*Top left: Creamware artist's paint box and cover (4"). Bottom: Chamber candlestick*
*gilded by Thomas Pardoe, the handle bearing his distinctive garter star. All Swansea, c. 1800.*

*Left: Swansea jug, decorated by Thomas Pardoe, dated 1803.*
*Right: Swansea jug, decorated and gilded by Thomas Pardoe, c.1800.*

*Swansea (Cambrian) plate. Vine leaf pattern. Black transfer, 1824-30.*

in style to those produced in Staffordshire, they are often taken as such. Originally in pairs, they each hold baskets and stand on rococo bases. These figures are unusual rather than rare but are not generally identified as Swansea because they are almost never marked, the very few recorded examples being marked CAMBRIAN in script. It may well be that these are so marked, despite not having been distinctively painted by Pardoe or Young (as is the case with all other items so marked), simply because the undersides of the little square bases are not big enough to accommodate the impressed SWANSEA mark. It now seems probable, on stylistic grounds, that a second, similar pair were also made at the Cambrian factory but none has so far been found with a mark. A similar attempt was made fifty years later, at the South Wales Pottery in Llanelli, to produce busts of Wesley but these too are so rare that it must be assumed that the technical problems were too great.

During this early period, the Pottery does not use factory marks and much of what is known has had to be deduced from the inscriptions. Fortunately, the habit of making individually inscribed pieces continued and is to be found on many early items whether they are hand-decorated or transfer-printed. A tea-jar, in salt-glaze, inscribed *M E Swansea potwork 1775*, can be regarded as the earliest known piece of marked Swansea. The hand-decoration on pieces from this early period is in cobalt blue or in what we term 'high temperature colours,' that is the greens, browns and yellows as found on 'Prattware'. This decoration is generally fairly simplistic, often

*Cambrian Monopteros pattern. Bevington period.*

depicting a house, flying a crossed pennant, in a landscape. It is certainly reminiscent of the decoration of Liverpool and is often mistakenly identified as such.

A help to the collector in identifying Swansea at this period is a peculiar arrangement of stilt marks. Stilts were the small pottery stands that were used to hold items apart in the kiln and they left small marks on the finished article. Usually, they had three feet, equidistantly spaced, which enabled them to sit snugly on the curved surface of the plate (on the three-legged milking-stool principle). For some reason, Swansea at this early time used four-footed stilts. These were not easy to use and often the potters would break off one leg. Thus, on Swansea pottery we see either four stilt-marks in a square or three, but in a right-angled triangle rather than a equilateral one. Both are very distinctive.

Thomas Rothwell and Thomas Pardoe were the most important of George Haynes' 'imports' during his partnership.

THOMAS ROTHWELL was an engraver of high repute who engraved copper-plates for early transfer-printed dinnerware, jugs, mugs etc from about 1790 to 1794. The quality of his work is second-to-none and although his work is never signed on pottery, we see fine examples bearing his name on paper and plaster in his views of Swansea. The transfers were used mainly in blue, or black/green but occasionally in

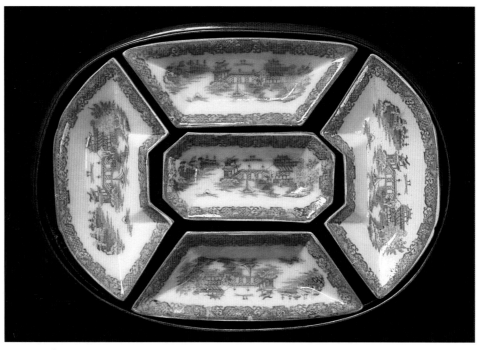

*Cambrian pickle or condiment set. Long Bridge pattern, c.1810.*

*Top right: Plate Long Bridge pattern. Top left: Plate hand-decorated in Pratt-type high temperature colours.*
*Bottom: Strainer, painted and gilded by Thomas Pardoe. All Cambrian, 1800-1810.*

*Examples from the two services made for
Miss Isabella Rowland of Llantrisant
by the Cambrian Pottery in the 1790's.*

*Cambrian jug with
transfer-decoration of a ship, c.1805.*

*Three examples of transfers by Thomas Rothwell on Cambrian Pottery:
Left: Jug Unity. Centre: Pickle dish, Elephant pattern.
Right: 'Fish Tin and Copper' commemorating Cornish trade (4¾").*

manganese. It is believed that he also painted pottery, but it is as an engraver that he will be remembered.

THOMAS PARDOE was by far the most important decorator of Swansea pottery. He arrived in Swansea in about 1795 and remained until 1809 when he moved to Bristol to set up his own painting *atelier*. During those fourteen years, his output was considerable. Although he is best-known for his botanical paintings, taken from Curtis' *Botanical Magazine*, his decoration is of great variety. Many of the sepia and/or green painted borders are attributed to him, but perhaps most importantly he decorated wonderful named ornithological plates, as well as landscape views of country houses. He was also a very highly-skilled gilder, and it is his distinctive 'garter'-type star which appears on Lord Nelson's service and elsewhere.

The other notable Swansea decorator of this period was WILLIAM WESTON YOUNG. He was to play a more important part in the history of Welsh ceramics through his association with Billingsly and Walker at Nantgarw. However, after an adventurous and financially precarious youth, Young moved, in 1802, to Wales, to Neath, where he farmed as tenant of John Llewellyn of Penllergaer, Lewis Weston Dillwyn's father-in-law. He was certainly known to be purchasing Swansea pottery at this time, perhaps for decorating at home, and it seems likely that he may have had experience of pottery decoration in Bristol. Thus, when his speculation in corn caused him to become bankrupt later in 1802, Young was able obtain employment at the Cambrian Pottery, where he arrived in early 1803. He stayed for about three years, and during this period he was involved with Dillwyn in illustrating the latter's book, *The British Confervae*. As a result of this, his output at the Pottery, predominantly paintings of butterflies, birds, animals, and occasionally landscapes, was relatively small and is now correspondingly sought-after.

POTTERY 'BODIES' DURING THE EARLY PERIOD

The two bodies, that is type of clay mixture, used at the Cambrian during this early period are creamware and 'fine white earthenware'.

The Cambrian creamware body is comparable with Wedgwood's Queen's Ware, which it unashamedly sought to imitate. It is light in weight, but not as light as Leeds ware, which Nance describes, with some prejudice, as 'too light'. Furthermore, the Swansea body is 'truer' in colour than many of its contemporaries, being less prone to yellowness.

The purity of this creamware provided a perfect canvas for Pardoe's decoration. It was, of course, used for many down-to-earth products which, because of their utilitarian nature, are less likely to have survived. Examples of creamware bidets and commode-chambers are known, and the Royal Institution collection has a fine cream-separator, as well as an artist's box. All are undecorated.

Creamware was sold both decorated and undecorated. Where decorated, it was very often by Thomas Pardoe. The breadth of his work was considerable. As well as the botanicals for which he is best known, Pardoe painted sepia landscapes, coloured landscapes, an ornithological series and, very occasionally, elaborate flower groups.

As well as the classical borders on more 'mass produced' ware, he was also responsible for overall geometric designs. The rims of creamware pieces of this time are usually lined in brown but are occasionally gilded on the more elaborately decorated pieces.

Swansea creamware tends to be marked and nearly always with SWANSEA impressed. Occasionally pieces are found bearing the mark *Cambrian* in script and, perhaps even more rarely the word *Swansea* in Pardoe's hand. This latter seems to occur on particularly well-painted pieces which happen to be on unmarked 'blanks'. Pardoe inscribed the name of the plant on the back of his botanicals in English only. Fortunately for today's collectors, his interrupted script is very distinctive and is most commonly found in brown and only very occasionally in green, blue or red.

It is important to remember that later, after Pardoe had left Swansea, the factory produced botanicals with a transferred outline filled in by hand. These have nothing of the quality of Pardoe's hand-painted botanicals and should not be mistaken for them.

The more ordinary white earthenware was usually decorated with transfer-prints from copper-plates by Thomas Rothwell, the most famous of these being the Swansea Long Bridge pattern. Other patterns include sailing-ships, the open chrysanthemum, and a variety of chinoiserie designs. Jugs in these patterns are often found inscribed with names and dates (also in transfer). Commonly, the rims of Swansea transfer-ware of this period are lined in yellow ochre. The transferred 'flat' wares are also more often marked than not, the mark again being SWANSEA impressed. Jugs, however, tend not to be marked. This white body was also decorated by hand in cobalt blue. A series of reddy-brown or black transfer plates depicting birds was made after the arrival of the Dillwyns and marked Dillwyn & Co.

A few items are recorded in black basalt, including the models of Anthony and Cleopatra referred to previously, as well as jugs and ink-wells. Cane-ware accounts for an even smaller number of recorded items. This body is a buff colour, is almost invariably unglazed, and lent itself well to elaborately moulded objects. Recorded shapes include game-pie dishes and elaborate vases.


PATTERNS (PRE-1811)

The idea of giving patterns set names and using these names by way of a factory mark had not come into being at this early period. Thus, many patterns have no name at all and others bear names given to them by collectors. Some pattern names are more 'established' than others. Most of the patterns of this period are the work of Thomas Rothwell. They include:

Long Bridge
Dagger Trophy
A Puzzle of Portraits
Moth Border Willow
Elephant Rocks
Open Chrysanthemum
Chinoiserie Palm
Fern Tree

*Selection of botanical paintings on Cambrian creamware by Thomas Pardoe, c.1800.*

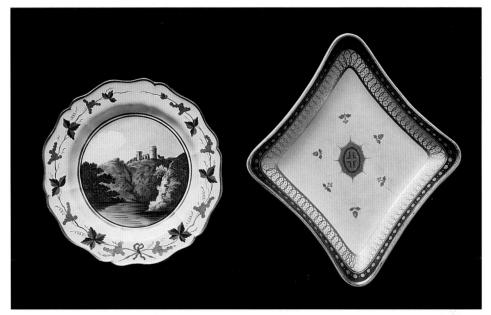

*Left: Dessert dish painted in sepia and gilded by Thomas Pardoe.*
*Right: Diamond-shaped dish from the service made for Lord Nelson, painted and gilded by Thomas Pardoe.*
*Both Cambrian Pottery, c.1800/1810.*

*Left: Cambrian mug in 'Puzzle of Portraits' pattern, c.1795.*
*Right: Cambrian blue transfer-printed jug from a copper-plate by Thomas Rothwell.*

## PATTERNS (1811-1817)

Willow pattern
Ships
Shells
Ornithological specimens
Cows Crossing a Stream
Fish Tin and Copper
Boy with Whip

## T. AND J. BEVINGTON (1817-1824)

When Lewis Weston Dillwyn retired in 1817, he suggested that the Bevingtons look for other partners rather than dispose of the business. The result was that George Haynes came back into partnership in the Pottery, along with his son, also George, and John Roby. Roby was a stranger to the area who had come from Warwickshire to join his brother-in-law's coal business and became a friend and neighbour to Haynes.

The arrangements for this new partnership were never really very successful and the partnership, throughout its life, was in almost continuous litigation with Dillwyn about the valuation of the business and stock of the pottery. Of course, throughout this period, he remained their landlord.

Things came to a head in 1821 when both the Haynes and Roby retired from the partnership, leaving the Bevingtons on their own. The 'and Co.' was then dropped from the firm's title, and father and son traded as T. & J. Bevington. These two men were equally unable to make the business work properly and, as soon as the lease expired, the Pottery reverted to Dillwyn.

During the time of both T. J. Bevington and Co. and T. & J. Bevington, it would appear that very little pottery was actually produced. Certainly, a very large amount of pottery 'in the white' had been taken over from Dillwyn & Co., and Nance believed that most items seen bearing dates for that period were made earlier and simply decorated by the Bevingtons. Very few innovative ideas occurred, and this is borne out by the fact that so little pottery is now seen bearing the mark 'Bevington and Co'. One of the few better known patterns to emerge during this period was Monopteros.

## THE SECOND DILLWYN PERIOD (1824-1831)

Control of the day-to-day working of the pottery reverted to the Dillwyn family in 1824. It may be that at this time Lewis Weston Dillwyn did attempt to sell the Pottery, but, equally, he had always kept open the option for one of his sons to enter the business. There was an agreement with Bevington and Co. that they would train any one of his sons, and that that son would be entitled to a partnership on his coming-of-age.

It is interesting to note here that the Bevingtons were legally represented at this time by John Jones, of Ystrad House, Carmarthen, the M.P. for Carmarthen, for whom the Pottery made commemorative mugs and jugs.

Since the Dillwyn family had taken control of the Pottery at the beginning of the century, the type of wares produced had been broadly similar. Once the pottery was back under Dillwyn's control in 1824, he undertook an improvement to the 'body' of his earthenware and generally improved the commercial appeal of the pottery's products. It is during this period that the majority of the items we find today were made.

A large number of hand-painted items were now produced. These range from simple stylised flowers to the elaborate pink-lustre birds and beasts on 'ribbon' plates. A number of individually inscribed and dated pieces also fall into this period. Cow-creamers, now so identified with Swansea pottery, were produced for the first time. These cows, sometimes rumoured to be used more for gin than for milk, were usually decorated with dabs of red and green colour and pink lustre, but other colours were also used, and even all-over brown or blue. More unusually, they were transfer decorated both on body and base, but otherwise the bases were generally grass-green painted over the glaze.

## PATTERNS (1824-1831)

The transfer patterns of this period are some of the best known.

> Cows Crossing a Stream *(a view supposed to be under Heathrow Airport)*
> Ladies with Baskets *(always blue on jugs, always black on plates)*
> The Ladies of Llangollen
> Castle
> Italian
> Ne Plus Ultra
> The Bridge at Lucano
> Pheasant
> Vine leaf
> Swiss Villa
> The Cheetah *(the most rare of all the standard Dillwyn transfers)*
> Black-and-white Eastern scenes and elaborate patterns of leaves and shells

Nursery-plates, too, are were very popular, with a variety of patterns, including the 'Seven Ages of Man' series.

## LEWIS LLEWELYN DILLWYN (1831-1850)

Lewis Llewelyn Dillwyn was the younger son of Lewis Weston Dillwyn. His elder brother John had inherited their maternal grandfather's estate at Penllergaer and, as a result, was to take the surname Llewelyn. This left Lewis Llewelyn Dillwyn to take over the Pottery, and this he did under his father's guidance in 1831, at the age of seventeen. The assignment was finally completed in 1836, but even thereafter the senior Dillwyn continued to take an active interest.

In 1837, Queen Victoria came to the throne, and the following year Lewis Llewelyn Dillwyn married Elizabeth, daughter of Henry De la Beche. De la Beche was a distinguished geologist and a director of the Museum of Practical Geology. The

*Four Cambrian Pottery puzzle jugs.*
*Left to Right: Long Bridge, Chrysanthemum, Pultney Bridge at Bath –*
*all c.1810, and a later pouch puzzle jug, (c.1830).*

*Left: Cambrian dessert plate painted with sepia view by William Weston Young,*
*the border and gilding by Thomas Pardoe.*
*Right: Cambrian supper dish base painted with a caracal by William Weston Young, (13½").*

*Three Cambrian puzzle jugs, c.1810.*

*Top: Plate from the series made for David Evans, Angel Inn, Carmarthen (10").*
*Right: Plate transfer-decorated in 'flow blue' Flower and Shell pattern.*
*Left: Plate transfer-decorated with Cows Crossing a Stream. All Cambrian, 1830/50.*

Museum took an interest in ceramics, and its collection later became a part of the Victoria and Albert Museum's collection. Obviously, Lewis Llewelyn Dillwyn had married a lady who shared his enthusiasm for his work.

During Lewis Weston Dillwyn's tenure, the pottery industry generally had polarised towards Staffordshire, and it was becoming more and more difficult to succeed in the outlying areas. This problem was more easily addressed at Llanelli by William Chambers, who, at this time, was starting from scratch. It was, however, something of a problem for the Cambrian.

In 1839, after long negotiations, the Dillwyns purchased the Glamorgan Pottery, sold off the stock and closed it down. This absorption of their main rival was only of short-term benefit because it provided the spare capacity and availability of skilled labour which was quickly taken up by William Chambers and was the catalyst which instigated the start of the South Wales Pottery at Llanelli. The Llanelly Pottery was to be the eventual downfall of the Cambrian Pottery and would outlive it by some fifty years.

At the Cambrian, less and less expensive hand-painted ware was being produced and more concentration placed on transfer-ware. However, a limited number of pouch-jugs, a shape introduced at this time, were well-painted with flower groups and often bear individual inscriptions. These pouch-jugs were the most popular shape of this era and are found in a variety of patterns and colours. They often bore the embossed mark 'Cymro Stone China' and this mark was unique to this particular shape. The pouch shape had a variation in the form of puzzle-jugs which themselves came with two differently shaped 'nipples' – one with a lion's head, the other with an eagle's head, and in two different sizes. All puzzle-jugs are rare, and these later Swansea examples are usually found decorated with Oriental-basket pattern.

As well as pouch-jugs, one of the most common of the factory's products at this time were octagonal jugs with simple stylised floral decoration and twig handles. These are sometimes found with a more robust hand painted-decoration and, even more unusually, in a transferred 'sheet' pattern.

PATTERNS (1831-1850)

> Cows Crossing a Stream
> Lazuli
> Ottoman *(regularly used on frog-mugs)*
> Hawthorn
> Amoy
> Whampoa
> Cuba
> Lady and Gallant
> Lady on Elephant
> Rhine
> Oriental basket
> Canton
> Named Views
> Portrait Series

A long series of nursery-plates was very popular at that time. They depicted various topographical views, usually of the West Country but also including a view of Swansea harbour. A similar series of 'Rural Scenes' is usually found on nursery-plates with a gadrooned rim which is more reminiscent of the Glamorgan factory.

Ship-plates are much associated with Swansea at this time. By now, the more elaborately engraved early-period ships had given way to the one design, found usually on plates but sometimes on jugs. Almost invariably found in black transfer, they appear from time to time in brown, and usually bear the factory mark *Dillwyn*, impressed.

Two interesting individual patterns are worthy of mention. Always printed in brown, they share a common border pattern and are inscribed in the centre of the plates *David Evans Angel Inn Carmarthen* and *John Daniel Cooper Carmarthen*. These were obviously made for pub use and are generally found on plates. A large beer-jug from the Angel Inn, and now in Carmarthen Museum, also depicts a standard ship transfer in brown.

Improved Saxon Blue is the name given to a small series of abstract patterns which were attempted during this period but without much success. These items, mainly tea-wares, are transfer decorated in a pale blue but did not manage to compete with the traditional darker colour. They usually bear a transferred mark *Dillwyn's Improved Saxon Blue*, in a circle.

The Coronation of Victoria resulted in some of the most sought-after examples of Swansea pottery, and this subject is dealt with in a separate chapter.

## DILLWYN'S ETRUSCAN WARE (1846/47-1850)

This is unquestionably the most interesting of the Pottery's products at this late date and is the last attempt by the Cambrian Pottery at producing a totally new pottery design. The shapes of all items of Etruscan Ware, with the exception of the candlesticks, spill vases, and the chamber candlestick, were taken from the Greek and were referred to by their Greek names. They are made from a red clay which was extracted from the Penllergaer estate of John Llewellyn (né Dillwyn, Lewis Llewelyn Dillwyn's brother), and they are decorated in transfer with designs taken from Greek originals by Mrs Dillwyn, and suitably interpreted by her. The technique involved 'glazing' the whole pot other than the transferred areas, and it would seem that this black glaze was painted on to the pot. It was suggested by Nance that the glaze was subject to oxidisation, causing a bloom on the black background. This may well be the case but it has recently been suggested to me that the discolouration so often found can result from the washing of Etruscan Ware. It should, in fact, be waxed.

Nance attributes eight different shapes to Etruscan Ware, as well as the wall brackets depicting a triton and a mermaid. This list is reprinted here verbatim:

1. The AMPHORA, with two upright handles, a high shoulder, narrow rim and bell-mouth, made apparently in one size only.
2. The PELIKE, with two upright handles, a sloping shoulder, and broad turned-over rim. Made in two sizes of slightly different shape

*Left: Cambrian moulded leaf plate, unusally decorated in transfer pattern – Swan and Flying Bird.*
*Right: Cambrian plate naively painted with bird on a pedestal, c.1830/50.*

*Six Cambrian child's plates, c.1830/40.*
*Fletcher, Teare, Wesley, Rural Scene, Swansea Harbour, one of the Seven Ages of Man series (largest 6½").*

*Right: Cambrian black transfer jug. Amoy pattern, c.1830.*
*Middle & Left: Typical Cambrian octagonal jugs with twig handles and hand-painted decoration, c.1830.*

*Right: Typical D. J. Evans period jug in Birds pattern.*
*Left: Strainer D. J. Evans Floral pattern (13¼").*
*Both Cambrian Pottery, 1860-70.*

3.  The KYLIX, or Tazza, a two-handled stem-cup. The handles are moulded on the form of a duck's wishbone, and there is only one shape and size.
4.  The OINOCHOE (jug), with upright handle and trefoil mouth, made also in only one shape and size.
5.  The PATERA, a deep plate. Of this, again, there is only one shape and size.
6.  Small vases of cylindrical form suitable for use as spill-holders. Of one size only.
7.  Small cylindrical boxes with covers, perhaps corresponding to certain forms of the greek PYXIS. Of one size only.
8.  Candlesticks of columnar form, made in at least two different sizes ($9^1/_8$" and $8^1/_4$"), of much the same shape.

To this list we can now add a small chamber-stick, the unique example of which was formerly in the author's collection and is now in the Glyn-Vivian Art Gallery in Swansea. This is clearly the most rare of the Etruscan series, closely followed by the small cylindrical box, or *pyxis*. This latter is very rare in itself, but I believe that there is only one example with its lid which is known. The history of this piece is worth noting. It first came to light in the sale at Chantry Acre, Bishopston, Swansea, the home of a member of the Vivian family. That day it was bought by Elis Jenkins, of Neath, who did so much for the study of Welsh ceramics and was a great Etruscan Ware enthusiast. The underbidder was the late Richie Maddock, one of the foremost collectors of Welsh ceramics. Many years later, it re-surfaced at the sale of the residue of Elis' collecton in Chester (having failed to make it to the main sale in London!), whence it was purchased by the author and was subsequently bought by the Glyn-Vivian Art Gallery along with the chamber-stick.

Etruscan Ware is marked 'Dillwyn's Etruscan Ware' in an elaborate black transfer cartouche. This mark is found in two different sizes.

A very scarce variation of Etruscan Ware is the one known example of the red body being overpainted in blue on an amphora in the collection of The Royal Institution of South Wales. Other related rarities are items of ordinary white ware decorated in green transfer from the copper-plates used for traditional Etruscan ware, and there is one known example, again in The Royal Institution collection, of an amphora transfer-decorated in Lazuli pattern.

By the 1840s, copper lustre (or more correctly, gold lustre) was very popular in Wales. However, very little was being produced either in Swansea or Llanelli because it was only really practicable to produce it on a terracotta body. The production of Etruscan Ware provided this body, and an experiment was conducted. The resulting copper lustre was very bright and shiny but obviously sold no better than the Etruscan Ware itself and presumably never got beyond the experimental stage. The only known examples are a very few *Oinochoe* or jugs.

Etruscan Ware would seem to have been the last attempt that Lewis Llewelyn Dillwyn made to produce goods that appealed to his own aesthetic taste. Clearly running a Pottery simply as a business did not really satisfy him and by 1850 he passed over the business of the Pottery to his manager, David Evans, and the senior traveller, John Evans Glasson. Nonetheless, he did retain the leases to the Pottery property.

## Evans and Glasson (1850-1861) and D. J. Evans and Co. (1861-1870)

"The ambitious days of the Cambrian Pottery had now gone for ever." Thus, Morton Nance describes the advent of the Pottery into the new post-Dillwyn era. There was never again to be any attempt to make anything out of the ordinary and for the remaining twenty years of its life the Pottery would produce very little of any merit, concentrating on pedestrian wares, largely for local use.

The original partnership was between David Evans, the manager of the Pottery, and John Evans Glasson, who had been a traveller for both The South Wales Pottery at Llanelli as well as for the Cambrian. It would appear that Glasson continued in this function, for even after becoming a partner he remained resident in Plymouth. There, he died in 1852 and the work of the Pottery was carried on by Evans alone until his son, D. J. Evans, became a partner in 1855. The firm continued to trade as Evans and Glasson until 1862, when David Evans finally retired and the trading name became D. J. Evans and Co.

The Pottery continued to go gradually downhill until in 1870 Lewis Llewelyn Dillwyn, who had retained the head lease, came to an arrangement with his sub-lease holders to close down the Pottery and sell the site to Cory, Yeo and Co. for a fuel works. It is an interesting aside to note that F. A. Yeo was Morton Nance's father-in-law.

The products of the factory at this period do little to stir the blood of the collector. Numerous patterns were still produced from the old Cambrian copper-plates including some of the West country views, 'Cows Crossing a Stream', Willow, and Oriental Basket. Amongst the new patterns of the period are Floral, with its convolvulus border, Googerat, Verandah, and a remake of Whampoa pattern printed in grey which probably represents the best quality transfer decoration of this period. This pattern, which has the mark *Whampoa D. J. Evans and Co Best Goods*, was not recorded by Nance and it would appear that all the known examples came from one dinner-service that came to light in the 1970s.

Perhaps the best-known pattern of the era was 'Birds', a series of views of birds, bought in from Staffordshire and used mainly on pear-shaped jugs with 'tinselling,' the over-decoration of transfer ware with a wash of transparent orange metallic lustre.

An attempt was made at this late stage to reintroduce the use of pink lustre but the decoration was very simplistic and the fact that so few pieces are known suggests that the experiment was not a success.

★   ★   ★

## Relationship with Swansea Porcelain (1814-1817)

The Swansea porcelain factory was, in effect, the Nantgarw Porcelain Works moved to Swansea where it could operate under the wing of Lewis Weston Dillwyn within the confines of the Cambrian Pottery. It was Dillwyn's wish to sacrifice, if necessary, the purity of the body in the interest of commercialism, and it was this that drove Billingsly and Walker back to Nantgarw.

*Left: Glamorgan Pottery ship plate (9"), c.1820.*
*Right: Cambrian Pottery ship plate (unusually with added initials) (10$\frac{1}{2}$"), 1830/50.*

*Left: Cambrian plate transfer-printed with*
*The Bridge at Lucano, c.1825.*
*Right: Cambrian plate transfer-printed with*
*very rare Cheetah pattern (10"), c.1825.*

*Dillwyn's Etruscan-ware Pelike (10"), c.1850.*

*Large Cambrian jug transfer-printed with the Pultney Bridge at Bath, c.1820/30.*

*Large Glamorgan creamware platter hand-decortaed in sepia (21$\frac{1}{2}$"), c.1815.*
*(Formerly in the collection of the late Neville Douglas-Jones).*

Considering the proximity of the factories and their relationship to Dillwyn, it is surprising that there is so little common ground between them. It is not within the remit of this guide to consider Swansea porcelain, a task that would, anyway, be better taken on by others, but it is worth mentioning the very limited common ground.

At least two transfer patterns appear to have been used on both pottery and porcelain. They are Tower pattern, a standard blue and white earthenware pattern that we always used to refer to as Castle Gatehouse, and Elephant pattern which was first engraved by Thomas Rothwell and which we always referred to as Elephant Rocks. Additionally, it seems likely that a design of shells and seaweed was also used on both pottery and porcelain.

There seems to have been even less common ground in shapes, the porcelain factory using different moulds. However, I have recently come across a pottery salmon dish painted to match the Marino Ballroom service. This service, made for the ballroom at Marino, Lord Swansea's mansion overlooking Swansea Bay, is unquestionably the ugliest service ever made of Welsh porcelain. Despite the fact that the decoration appears to be a filled in transfer, it is in fact entirely hand-decorated and clearly his lordship was in need of fish platters not found in porcelain.

## *Marks on Cambrian Pottery*

1764-1783 – No marks as such occur during this period, although a few items have been found with writen identification, e.g. 'Made in Swansea' on the base of an inscribed jug.

1783-1810

| | | |
|---|---|---|
| SWANSEA | The standard mark of the period |  |
| CAMBRIAN | Painted | |
| SWANSEA | Painted | |

1802-1817
DILLWYN & CO — Impressed

1810-1811
DILLWYN CAMBRIAN
POTTERY SWANSEA — impressed in two circles

1811-1817
DILLWYN & CO SWANSEA — impressed horseshoe

DILLWYN & CO SWANSEA      printed in a circle
(only on Wellington jugs)

1817-1824
BEVINGTON & CO      impressed

1824-1850
DILLWYN & CO      impressed horseshoe

DILLWYN      impressed in a crescent

DILLWYN (over) SWANSEA      impressed in a crescent

1836-1850
DILLWYN SWANSEA      in a crescent

CYMRO STONE CHINA      raised cartouche

Transfer pattern marks incorporating the name
Dillwyn or D & Co.
'Dillwyn's Improved Saxon Blue'      printed in a circle

1850-1862
EVANS & GLASSON

EVANS & GLASSON SWANSEA      impressed in a triangle

EVANS & GLASSON SWANSEA      printed
BEST GOODS

1862-1870
DAVID EVANS
D J EVANS & CO      both printed in conjunction with a
pattern name

*Two pierced-edge or ribbon plates, c.1820/30.*
*Right: Cambrian.     Left: Glamorgan.*

*Right: Glamorgan transfer-decorated cow creamer, c.1830.*
*Left: Cambrian hand-decorated cow cream in pink lustre and red on green enamelled base, c.1830.*

*Left: Glamorgan jug transfer-decorated with rural scenes, c.1820/30.*
*Right: Similar shaped jug from the Cambrian factory, Amoy pattern. (Note distinctive handle shape), 1825/30.*

*Left: Llanelly 'Experimental Ware' jug after the original by Wedgwood in Gothic taste.*
*Centre: Llanelly Glamorgan-shaped jug, blue experimental body with sprigging.*
*Right: Llanelly Drabware jug, Raglan shape. Largest 8¹/₂" – all c.1840/45.*

*Left: Llanelly octagonal jug with snake handle, after Masons, Bombay Japan pattern.*
*Centre: Llanelly Glamorgan-shape jug, Oriental pattern.*
*Right: Llanelly Penhale shape jug, hand-decorated.*
*Largest 7¹/₄". All 1840/55.*

# The Glamorgan Pottery
## 1813-1839

THE COLLECTOR HAS NEVER regarded the products of the Glamorgan Pottery in quite the same light as the early work of the Cambrian Pottery, but in recent times there has come about a new appreciation of the quality of Glamorgan Pottery.

George Haynes' partnership with Lewis Weston Dillwyn finally came to an end in 1810, and Haynes left the Cambrian Pottery. During the subsequent two years, a new partnership was formed between William Baker, Thomas Irwin, and four members of the Bevan family: William Sn., William Jnr., Robert and Martin. William Baker was George Haynes' son-in-law and had been his assistant at the Cambrian. Haynes was never himself a shareholder in the Glamorgan Pottery but was very much the power behind it. Certainly it was his expertise and experience that enabled the pottery to be started and caused the interest of the Bevan family in the venture. The enterprise was basically a partnership between the Baker/Haynes family and the Bevan family, Irwin being the son-in-law of William Bevan Senior.

The Pottery started production in 1813 or 1814 but suffered a severe blow when, in 1819, William Baker died. The loss of such an experienced partner necessitated the appointment of a manager, and Evan Davies was appointed, with Richard Davies as his assistant, which allowed the production to continue without change. In 1830, George Haynes died, and, at about the same time, the Bevan family's main business, the Landore Iron Co., went into liquidation. Some of the Bevan family's shares in the pottery were offered for sale but, in the event, were redistributed amongst the family. However, from this time on the partnership would have been quite pleased to have sold the business.

At the end of 1837, Lewis Weston Dillwyn agreed to purchase the Glamorgan Pottery, and by the end of 1838 he had done so and closed it down. The advantages of this closure to the new South Wales Pottery at Llanelli will be considered in the chapter on Llanelly Pottery.

It is an interesting aside that Dillwyn, not having any use for the Glamorgan premises (the Cambrian already having enough space) offered it to Brameld and Co , the manufacturers of Rockingham Porcelain, as a porcelain works but only on the understanding that they made only translucent porcelain which, presumably, he saw as no threat to his earthenware business. The offer was not taken up as Brameld already had their own financial problems.

The Glamorgan Pottery usually referred to its body as Opaque China, an attempt to suggest that although not 'china' in the accepted sense (that is not translucent porcelain) it was nonetheless of superior quality. They used this term as part of their standard printed mark. The expression was one that George Haynes was fond of,

*Glamorgan Pottery.*
*Top: Floral spray. Left: The Ladies of Llangollen. Right: Castle Gatehouse. (All blue transfer).*

having first used it to describe the fine early Cambrian body for which he was responsible, although the Cambrian never marked their pottery Opaque China.

The Glamorgan Pottery is perhaps best remembered for the quality of its transfer ware. A wide variety of patterns was used, and some of these were identical to those produced by the Cambrian, perhaps the best-known of these being the 'Ladies of Llangollen'. The examples from the Glamorgan factory are superior to those of the Cambrian, and it may well be that the Cambrian used the copper-plates of the Glamorgan after they had taken it over. Other 'standard' Glamorgan blue transfer designs include 'Cottage Girl', 'Haymaker', 'Harper', the rather rare 'Campania', and a sheet pattern, much used, called 'Vine'. Additionally, a pattern in a paler blue depicting simple sprays of leaves and flowers was popular for dinner and dessert services.

Black, as well as brown, transfers were a characteristic of the Glamorgan factory, particularly on jugs and teawares. These include English rural views, sometimes with fishing scenes, and also of Swiss views. Very occasionally, these are found with inscriptions, which are usually in brown. The illustrated example is inscribed *Eliz th Jones Born March 6th 1832*, and this example is printed in brown. However, sometimes the printing can be in purple, and this is usually the case for the jugs made for the Reform Act of 1832, an event much celebrated by Glamorgan Pottery. The shape of Elizabeth Jones' jug is the most common form from Glamorgan and was later copied by the South Wales Pottery, where we refer to it as the 'Glamorgan shape' – the only difference being in the shape of the handle.

*Left: Llanelly plate in Amherst Japan pattern, overpainted, 1840-55.*
*Right: Llanelly plate in Damask border pattern, 1840-55.*

*Four Llanelly child's plates:*
*Top: Father Matthew. (6½")*
*Left & Right: Pair depicting children at play.*
*Bottom: Japan pattern with typical molded border. All 1840-55.*

*Three Llanelly toy plates (2³/₄"): Top Left: View of Conway Bridge. Top Right: Clock-face with William Chambers mark. [Note: these two prints are most commonly found on copper-lustre clock-face jugs]. Bottom: Rare name plate. All 1840-45.*

*Left: Llanelly Milan pattern meat plattern – unusually printed in puce. (13¹/₂"), 1840-55. Right: Llanelly Coombes & Holland plate – Flora pattern, c.1855-60.*

The Glamorgan had its own prints for ship-plates, these being much more elaborate than the later Cambrian ships and, in fact, much more reminiscent of the early Cambrian examples. Very unusually, these are marked by the inclusion of the letters GP Co S within the design itself.

Glamorgan cow-creamers are very similar in shape to those made at the Cambrian factory. The difference appears to be in the shape of the head (the Glamorgan cows having a wider and flatter forehead) and in the length of the neck. The decoration of Glamorgan cows is usually black transfer of country views. They are found with painted decoration but much less often than has been commonly thought. It now seems likely that the cows illustrated in Nance and described as pink lustre are in fact Cambrian, and that the Glamorgan pottery did not use pink lustre at all. The tail of the Glamorgan cow is taller than that of the Cambrian, reaching the body of the cow almost vertically and behind the saddle, whereas the tail of the Cambrian cow is flatter and meets the body directly under the saddle.

Much has been made of the quality of Cambrian Pottery creamware. The Glamorgan pottery also made creamware, although it only came into being right at the end of the period associated with British creamware. Only two pieces are recorded. They are both large meat platters painted with an elaborate, somewhat oriental, scene of birds in trees, in a sepia palette. They would certainly have been part of a service but no other items are recorded. Being hand-decorated they bear an impressed mark 'Baker Bevans and Irwin' in a horseshoe.

Green ware was popular throughout the Britain in the first quarter of the nineteenth century and the Glamorgan produced some of the very best. As was usual, all were leaf based, some stylised, but the best Glamorgan examples are very naturalistic. Unlike the Cambrian Pottery, which used green glazes for a variety of wares, the Glamorgan only made leaf shaped dessert services.

## Marks on Glamorgan Pottery

All marks of the Galmorgan Pottery are based on the names or initials of the proprietors Baker Bevans and Irwin, the printed marks usually incorporating the words OPAQUE CHINA.

BAKER BEVANS & IRWIN                          impressed in a horseshoe


BAKER BEVANS & IRWIN SWANSEA                  impressed in a horseshoe


OPAQUE CHINA BB&I                             Printed


AN IMPRESSED 'PRINCE OF WALES' FEATHERS (impressed) is used with or without the impressed Baker Bevans & Irwin Swansea impressed mark.

# Llanelly Pottery
## 1839-1922

AS WE HAVE SEEN, the Glamorgan Pottery was eventually, and perhaps inevitably, absorbed by Dillwyn's Cambrian Pottery and ceased producion in the latter part of 1838. This provided a catalyst for William Chambers Junior, the son of the 'Lord of the Manor' of Llanelli, a small town some ten miles to the West. William Chambers Senior had inherited the estate of Llanelli from the Stepney family, who had been the primary land-owners in the town for some generations. His son was a pillar of local society, sitting on the bench and involving himself in many (if not most) affairs of Government and business in the town.

William Chambers Jnr saw in the closure of the Glamorgan Pottery the opportunity for a new business venture which would, additionally, benefit the people of the town. The new Pottery was built during 1839 and a certain amount of plant was bought from the Glamorgan Pottery. A number of key-workers also moved to Llanelli but undoubtedly the most important asset from the Glamorgan Pottery to find its way to the new enterprise was its designs.

In the early years of the Pottery, the shapes and patterns of the products often bore a marked resemblance to those of the Glamorgan. There was no way in which a business could protect designs, and so shapes and patterns were often stolen from competitors, or brought in with the workers who moved from one pottery to another. This practice was much to Llanelly's advantage when it came to selling their wares. However, it should be noted that the actual moulds and copper-plates from the Glamorgan Pottery were not used, and indeed it would have been surprising if Dillwyn would have been prepared to sell such things to his new rival now that he owned the Glamorgan Pottery plant.

Unquestionably, the most influential of the new employees to come from Swansea was William Bryant. He had worked in the pottery industry in Swansea for some 26 years, being a clerk in the Cambrian Pottery as early as 1812, and latterly as agent to the Glamorgan Pottery, and was thus of great value in Llanelli. He arrived in the middle of 1840 by which time the Pottery was just starting production. Full production was not really under way until the latter part of 1841, when the majority of the workers' contracts were signed. Many of these are in the collection of the Royal Institution in Swansea.

---

*Note:* The South Wales Pottery. Confusion can arise when the term South Wales Potteries is used to refer to all the factories of the area, as this was the specific name of the factory at Llanelli throughout its life and more specifically during the first period (1839-1855), when all marked pieces of Llanelly bear the name South Wales Pottery.

We have also chosen to continue Dilys Jenkins' convention of spelling Llanelli thus when the town is referred to, but Llanelly when referring to the pottery or its products.

*Left: Inscribed 7¹/₂" jug with religious scene.*
*Centre: Avis pattern (7¹/₂").   Right: Etruria pattern.*
*All Llanelly, c.1880.*

*Selection of Llanelly items hand-decorated in Persian Rose pattern, c.1880/1900.*

*Early period Llanelly candlestick (11"), c.1840/45, flanked by two late period candlesticks, hand-decorated by Samuel Shufflebotham, c.1910.*

*Llanelly Chestnut basket and stand hand-decorated with tea roses and Spill vase hand-decorated with wild roses – all by Shufflebotham, c.1910.*

43

*Llanelly Pottery.*
*Left: Jersey scene in black with Lavinium border in blue, c.1865. Right: Lahore pattern in blue, c.1850.*

The Pottery was to remain in the control of William Chambers Jnr until 1855, when his father died. This event precipitated a situation that remains a mystery to this day. It came to light that William Chambers Senior was not married to the mother of his children, despite having described her, on her memorial in Llanelli Parish Church, as 'my dear wife'. The reason for this is not known but obviously there must have been a substantial bar to their marriage, for Chambers Sen. would have been aware that this would preclude his son from retaining the Stepney estate. The Stepney family were already aware of the situation and as soon as Chambers Sen died they took action to regain the estate.

William Chambers Jnr very quickly left the town after receiving elaborate valedictory gifts from the townspeople. However, his father had created numerous long leases in his favour and it took many years of litigation with the Stepneys to sort out the position. It has recently been established that, as part of the agreement, William Chambers Jr. retained a head lease on the pottery for many years after he left Llanelli.

The South Wales Pottery was a typical early Victorian pottery, and, during the fifteen years of this Chambers period, it produced a wide variety of wares very largely for everyday use. Perhaps the most interesting product from an academic point of view is a very small number of lithophanes (moulded porcelain transparencies). Although German lithophanes are comparatively common, few British manufacturers attempted to make them and it seems that none of the factories which produced them (primarily Wedgwood, Minton and Beleek) had much success with them. Lithophanes are the only recorded examples of porcelain produced at Llanelli. It really is a remarkable anomaly that a factory of this nature should produce such technically difficult items at all. The final irony is that the known marked examples bear the legend 'South Wales *Pottery*'.

PATTERNS 1840-1855 (CHAMBERS PERIOD)

The following are the most often recorded patterns:
   Damask Border
   Milan
   Colandine
   Bombay Japan
   Amherst Japan
   Oriental
   Willow
   Panorama

Other less common patterns include:
   Lazuli
   Woodbine
   Botanical
   Giraffe
   Persian Rose *(not to be confused with later hand-painted Persian Rose )*
   Syria
   Syrius *(using the copper-plates of Calland's short-lived pottery at Landore)*
   Swiss Sketches

Hand-painting during this period tends to be restricted to infill of transfer patterns, but some use of freehand painting is known – simply of a stylised leaf pattern. Some use was also made of sponge decoration in this early period, both all over blue, and also a more formal 'potato print' type of decoration. This latter was to become one of the pottery's main products fifty years later, but is extremely unusual in this early period.

COPPER LUSTRE

As with the Swansea potteries, copper lustre (or more correctly gold lustre) is extremely rare. Staffordshire copper lustre has always been popular in Wales and, as a result, is often associated, incorrectly, with the Welsh potteries.

   In Llanelli, the only known examples of copper lustre are clock-face jugs and those *all* bear the name William Chambers Jnr on the clock face, where one would expect to find the clock-maker's name. Often, but not always, the lustre is of poor quality, looking somewhat brown.

EXPERIMENTAL BODIES

An interesting series of rarities from the early years of the Pottery occasionally turn up. These are a limited number of items in a small variety of body colours. It is the clay which is coloured rather than applying a colour over a white body. The colours recorded are two varieties of blue, a drabware body and another somewhere between these two. All are used for fairly elaborate shapes which then need no further deco-

*Pair of Llanelly jugs depicting Jersey scenes, c.1900.*

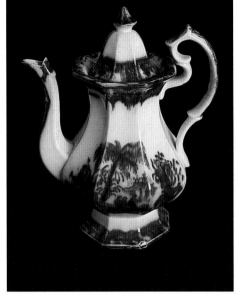

*Ynysmeudwy coffee pot of large size (12¹/₄")*
*decorated with Rio pattern in flow blue, c.1850.*

*Llanelly plate (10") depicting Marie Jones, a spill-vase decorated with cherries, and a tall vase with irises.*
*All hand-decorated by Shufflebotham, c.1910.*

*Ynysmeudwy toilet bowl*
*transfer-decorated Rural pattern, c.1860.*

*Cambrian mug commemorating the coronation*
*of Queen Victoria (3") and a matching plate*
*depicting Prince Albert, probably made*
*the time of their wedding, 1837 and 1840.*

*Left: Cambrian Pottery jug (6¹/₂) transfer-decorated with an anti-Napolean cartoon, c.1815.*
*Right: Similar jug, decorated in red transfer on canary yellow with the*
*other known anti-Napoleon cartoon, c.1815.*

*Llanelly Pottery.*
*Left: Colandine pattern in blue, c.1860. Right: Gower pattern in purple, c.1860.*

ration. At the same time, these shapes are very largely, but with a few exceptions, only found in the experimental bodies. The variety of both shapes and colours found within this very small group of pots suggests that they were part of a design experiment.

SHAPES

Most of the items produced at Llanelli were for everyday use and the shapes were, in the main, similar to those use by the Staffordshire factories of the period. The influence of the Glamorgan Pottery can be seen in many shapes, although the actual moulds were not used. Some shapes were directly copied from other potteries, as is the case with the rare gothic shape much more frequently found made by Wedgwood. Two varieties of tall candlesticks are known. They are both found undecorated but embossed, one with daisy heads and the other with vine tendrils – occasionally picked out in blue.

A few items are somewhat outside the run of production of many potteries, notably bed-pans and feeding-cups, but these were extremely rare. The National Museum of Wales has a bust of Wesley, in the Staffordshire manner, marked *South Wales Pottery* and this is probably a direct copy from a Staffordshire model. Simlarly, a cow-creamer is recorded, marked *SWP*, and this is identical in every way to the Swansea examples, but is just a shade smaller. This suggests that it came from a mould taken directly from a Swansea cow, which then shrank slightly in firing.

Overall, the products of the factory were of a high standard and the variation and diversity of the wares make this an exciting period for the collector, particularly as this period has been somewhat neglected of late in favour of the rather brighter, but less technically interesting, twentieth-century period. Llanelly Pottery must be one of the few factories whose products become more valuable the newer they are!

COOMBS AND HOLLAND PERIOD (1855-1858)
AND W. T. HOLLAND PERIOD (1858-1875)

When William Chambers left Llanelli in 1855, he retained a long lease of the Pottery site and sub-let the business to Messrs Coombs and Holland. This partnership was to be short-lived, soon getting into financial trouble. As a result, the lease was surrendered to Chambers in 1858.

Chambers entered into a new agreement with William Holland, who then carried on the business alone. However, the plant was still used and, as far as shapes and patterns were concerned, the departure of Coombs had little effect. It even seems likely that the mark C&H continued to be used after Coombes' departure on patterns that were already in production beforehand. William Holland continued on his own until 1868, and then with David Guest until 1875, when the Pottery came into severe financial difficulties and ceased to trade.

The twenty years of Holland's ownership of the pottery are the most workmanlike period of the pottery's life. The actual 'body' of the items was of the best quality and the transfer-printing was of a very high standard, being particularly suited to the hard bodies. Very little hand-painting was employed, except for simple borders, although hand-painted inscriptions were first introduced at this time. The body was also improved to an ironstone, and some examples are marked IRONSTONE (impressed). Some patterns, notably Llanelly Bouquet and Flora, were registered by Llanelly and used exclusivly there. The latter, which is, in fact, a series of different floral patterns, was exhibited by the Pottery at the exhibition of 1861 and is the only Welsh pattern to be found bearing the diamond-shaped registration lozenge (in transfer). It is interesting that the Llanelly Pottery was exhibiting at this prestigious exhibition when the Cambrian was not.

PATTERNS OF THE WILLIAM HOLLAND PERIOD

Colandine
Llanelly Bouquet
Nautillus
Fern
Rural
Jersey Scenes
Livinium
Albert
Avis *(A direct attempt to copy the Swansea David Evans 'Birds' pattern)*
Gower
Etruria
This is Jack's birthday and The Young Charioteer
Alhambra *(Also used at Ynysmeudwy)*
Ivy Wreath
Entente Cordiale *(A pattern produced either at Llanelly or Ynysmeudwy, or even both)*
Moss Rose

*Llanelly Pottery.*
*Left: Syria pattern. Right: Eastern pattern. (Both brown transfers), c.1880.*

Bryncaerau  *(A rare pattern probably produced only for Bryncaerau House which was the home of C. W. Coombs and now houses Llanelly Borough Council's collection of Llanelly pottery)*

A variety of wares was produced at this time, but of a practical rather than decorative nature. The main products were table-wares in the form of dinner-services, jugs, and toilet-wares. Even such large items as foot-baths were produced, although it would seem only in small quantities.

### THE FINAL PERIOD (1877-1922)

After closing in 1875, the Pottery was resurrected in 1877 by two cousins who had long previous experience of the industry. David Guest, who had been in partnership with William Holland since 1868, was the son of a potter who had come to Llanelli as early as 1841 (and signed one of the original contracts of employment). His cousin Richard Dewsberry came down from Staffordshire to become his partner. By 1906, however, both these partners had died, and Richard Guest, David Guest's son, became sole proprietor of the Pottery. In 1912, the business became a company, with the shares held by the Guest family, but by 1922 the writing was on the wall and, despite attempts to revive interest, the pottery was forced to close.

During the first years of the Guest and Dewsberry partnership, the products were very much utilitarian and of poor quality. There were no new patterns. However, by the 1890s a new wave of hand-painting began which was to create a swansong which, although insufficient to pull the company through the recession of the 1920s, nonetheless gave us those exciting items for which Llanelli is best-known by collectors.

At first, this was mainly in the form of sponged decoration. This method had been used in the early days of the factory and involved placing paint on to the 'biscuit' pot with a sponge. A refinement in this late period (and a technique widely used throughout the British pottery industry) was the application of the paint with the hard root of the sponge, carved into an intricate shape. The root was hard enough to form a distinct shape but absorbent enough to enable the pattern to be repeated identically many times over – and very quickly.

At the same time, loose, brightly coloured hand-painting came into vogue. This now seems very modern in style to us and must have been very much more so at the time. Mass-produced as a standard pattern, it probably had no name, but which Dilys Jenkins chose to call Persian Rose

During the early years of the 20th century, these two techniques were brought together to form the most lasting image of Llanelly Pottery – the cockerel plate. These were decorated with a naive cockerel, surrounded by a sponged border. They were painted very largely by Sarah Roberts (*Auntie Sal*), but probably by other painters and certainly visiting school-children as well.

Transfer-ware was, of course, still in production, the main patterns being Asiatic Pheasant, Willow, and continuations of such patterns as Llanelly Bouquet.

## SAMUEL SHUFFLEBOTHAM

The last great event of Llanelly Pottery's life was the arrival of Samuel Shufflebotham. He came from Bristol where he learned the skill of painting flowers on pottery, almost certainly from George Stewart, who had himself learned the technique at Wemyss. We do not know exactly when he arrived but he was married in Bristol in 1908 and it seems likely that he came to Llanelli soon afterwards. We know that he left in 1915.

During this short period, he painted a wide variety of subjects, but mainly flowers and fruit. Roses were by far and away the most common and perhaps Greengages the most rare. Plums, Cherries, Apples, Pansies, Irises, Poppies, Daffodils (in both yellow and green), Palm leaves, Hibiscus, Tulips, Blackberries and Fuchsias make up the rest.

Large bowls decorated with a view of Llanelli Parish Church are the most important of Shufflebotham's subjects but, in addition to fruits and flowers, numerous others are found. These include Cocks and Hens, Storks, Dutch Children, Puritans, Ships, Watermills and Cottages, and even Mari Jones with her Bible striding across the pottery.

Many shapes are found decorated only by Shufflebotham. Rose bowls, square-handled vases and three-handled 'Art Noveau' style vases, cabaret sets and candlesticks. However, the most interesting aspect is that Shufflebotham had his own 'body'. The pottery body on which his hand-painting was carried out differed from the everyday body of the pottery in that it is a much more creamy colour and thus a much 'gentler' canvas for his brightly coloured subjects. Never is the work of Shufflebotham found on other than this creamy body, and indeed never is the creamy body found decorated other than by Shufflebotham. It should, however, be noted that some shapes are made in both bodies and decorated accordingly. Perhaps the best examples of this are the chestnut baskets and stands which have always been assumed to have been designed and made by George Henshall.

During this late period, mocha ware was made in prodigious quantities for the pub trade. Pubware mocha is very common from many factories and is almost never blessed with a factory mark. Thus, the only clue to the factory is by the assay office's sand-blasted mark. This is a good guide but not a definitive indication of the origin of the pots. Llanelli Assay office used the number 458.

After Shufflebotham left Llanelli in 1915, the factory limped on for a few more years, but in 1922 the Pottery fired its last kiln. With its closure came the end of over 150 of commercial pottery production in South Wales.

## Marks on Llanelly (South Wales) Pottery

### 1839-1855 – WILLIAM CHAMBERS JNR. PERIOD

All marks of this period, whether impressed or printed, are based on the factory name 'South Wales Pottery'.

SOUTH WALES POTTERY                                    impressed in a horseshoe

SOUTH WALES POTTERY                                    impressed in two circles
     W C JUN

SOUTH WALES POTTERY                                    impressed in two circles
     W Chambers

SOUTH WALES POTTERY                                    impressed

WILLIAM CHAMBERS JUNIOR                                impressed
     SOUTH WALES POTTERY
          LLANELLY

SWP                                                    impressed

Various printed pattern marks incorporating
South Wales Pottery or SWP

## 1855-1875 – COOMBES & HOLLAND AND W. T. HOLLAND PERIOD

All marks in this period are entirely printed in conjunction with the pattern mark with the exception of an impressed mark IRONSTONE CHINA which is used on its own, whether the piece bears any other mark or not.

Although Coombs retired very soon after the commencement of his partnership with Holland, it seem certain that the C&H mark continued to be used by Holland alone for patterns that had first been used (and thus the copper plates made) during Coombs' time at the pottery.

C&H                                          printed
WTH                                          printed

## 1877-1922 – GUEST & DEWSBERRY PERIOD

Factory marks were only used in this period on transfer-decorated items in conjunction with the pattern mark, and on items of the late 'creamy' body. Other hand-painted items such as Persian Rose or Cockerels are never marked. The mark used on transfer wares is G & D with or without the initial 'L'.

Items of 'creamy body' are marked LLANELLY, LLANELLY POTTERY or LLANELLY ART POTTERY in black stencil. A smaller mark LLANELLY in a slight curve and in green is found on the better painted items and it might well be that this mark was exclusive to Shufflebotham. Three other *very rare* printed marks are found on 'creamy' items:

1. An oval stamp – GUEST & DEWSBERRY SOUTH WALES POTTERY. This is printed in green and appears to be an office stamp.
2. Two circles enclosing a spray of daffodils surrounded by the words Y GEN-INEN NWYDDAU CYMRU.
3. A dragon surrounded by two daffodils and the words LLANELLY POTTERY WALES.

Additionally, occasionally items painted by Shufflebotham are marked LLANELLY in green in his hand.

## SIGNED ITEMS

Llanelly Pottery items are not generally signed but a few items decorated by Shufflebotham bear the initials SWS (Samuel Walter Shufflebotham). These items would appear to have been given to friends and relatives by Shufflebotham rather than sold by the pottery.

One item of Llanelly pottery is known inscribed on the base 'Painted by W. Harvey 1913'. No other reference to this painter has been found.

# Minor Factories

## CALLANDS POTTERY, LANDORE
### 1852-1856

CALLANDS POTTERY AT LANDORE was a very-short lived venture that began in September, 1852. Its preliminary advertising stated that 'earthenware of every variety is manufactured.' James Hinkley, who had been Lewis Llewelyn Dillwyn's manager at the Cambrian Pottery, was the agent for Callands, which would have been a great benefit to them. However, times were not good for the pottery industry and Callands factory was offered for sale as early as mid-1853, before it was a year old. Another attempt to let the premises was made in 1855 and the following year it was let for an unrelated purpose.

The main pattern for which Callands is known is Syria. A fine example of the high quality of goods which the factory was able to produce is found in a multi-colour transfer-decorated 'exhibition' jug in the Swansea Museum. They are also known to have produced Willow pattern. However, very little marked Callands comes to light. Marked examples of Sirius pattern are marked in transfer *Callands Swansea* above and below the pattern name. Interestingly, the copper-plates for Sirius were to end up at Llanelli, where the words Calland Swansea are scoured out on the copper-plate to leave the pattern name with two thick lines above and below. It appears that no impressed marks were used.

## THE DYVATTY STREET POTTERY
### (Pleasant Vale Pottery) 1843-1892

Very little is known about this pottery despite its comparatively long life. It would appear to have been started in about 1843 by one William Mead, a potter from Bovey Tracey, who came to Swansea to work at the Cambrian, and continued until 1892.

It is probable that the main products of this pottery were industrial and simple red earthenware items for domestic use. It certainly seems unlikely that any form of decoration as such was attempted. Game-jugs, elaborately moulded with hares and other game and glazed in a thick, dark brown glaze (usually referred to as Rockingham glaze), have always been attributed to this factory but it now seems unlikely that they were made there. Certainly, game-jugs of the type believed to be Dyfatty were made at Llanelli (and marked SOUTH WALES POTTERY), and presumably in Staffordshire.

The late John Bunt, formerly curator of the Glyn-Vivian Art Gallery, was able to examine the contents of a drain that was unearthed on the site of the Pottery (late one evening while dressed in a dinner jacket) and found some small unglazed animals which would appear to be toys or small ornaments. No marked items have been recorded.

*Ynysmeudwy Pottery.*
*Left: An unusual inscribed plate. Right: Oriental Birds pattern in blue.*

# YNYSMEUDWY POTTERY
## 1845-1875

The pottery at Ynysmeudwy came into being in 1845 when it was opened as a brick-works by two brothers Michael Martyn Williams and William Williams. By 1849, it had taken on the character of a traditional Victorian pottery making a variety of table wares, jugs and childs' plates. William Williams carried on alone from 1856 to 1859 and was then, in turn, superceded by Charles Williams, another brother, for just one year.

From 1860 until 1869 the factory was owned by Griffith Lewis and John Morgan, owners of the Primrose Colliery at Pontardawe. In 1869 John Morgan died and in 1871 Griffith Lewis sold out to W. T. Holland, the owner of Llanelly Pottery. Holland then removed the plant that was of use to him to Llanelli and continued to run Ynysmeudwy as a manufactory of bricks, chimney pots, garden ornaments and pipes etc. During this short period, up to 1875 when the Llanelly pottery was forced to close briefly, some of the Ynysmeudwy patterns and shapes continued to be used at Llanelly.

The body of Ynysmeudwy pots, while not comparable to that of the early Cambrian wares, was of reasonable quality, and the standard of some of the transfer ware was very high. Some very creditable items were made, most particularly, a fine, pierced chestnut-basket which is now in the Royal Institution, and a very ambitious large coffee-pot marked Williams in 'flow blue' Rio pattern. Flow blue was a technique widely used in the ceramic industry in early Victorian times. The blue transfer was allowed to bleed into the glaze on a pot giving the transfer a very blurred effect, and causing the glaze itself to take on a blue hue. It obviously proved as popular then as it does with today's collectors.

Many of the patterns employed during the early period, pre-1856, such as Rio, Gem, Ivy, Alhambra, Rural and Oriental Birds, continued to be used throughout the life of the Pottery and were eventually amongst those patterns taken over by Holland. Later, between 1856 and 1860 Flora, Wreath, Chantrey and Alma were added to the range. Finally, during the time of Lewis and Morgan's ownership Livinium, Asiatic Pheasant, Vase, Anemone, Priory, Star, and perhaps the best known, Woodbine were introduced. Many of these were used by Holland at Llanelli and it now seems most probable that Holland did not use his W.T.H. mark, typical of Llanelly, in Ynysmeudwy. Where this mark is found on typically Ynysmeudwy patterns it was added to the copper-plates when they were used at Llanelly.

This question of the overlap between Llanelly and Ynysmeudwy does seem to have caused difficulties for students of Welsh pottery for some time. The answer seems to be that Holland produced no pottery of a domestic, decorated, type at Ynysmeudwy, but did make use of the Ynysmeudwy moulds and patterns in Llanelli. Some patterns became standard to Llanelly, but are more rare than the established Llanelly patterns, and it may be that they were made as replacements only. These patterns are sometimes (although rarely) marked WTH, but this would appear to have been added to the copper-plate. Examples of patterns so marked include Oriental Birds and Anemone. From time to time, one comes across parts of Ynysmeudwy patterns used at Llanelli such a Livinium's border pattern which is sometimes found used instead of the shell border on Llanelly Jersey Scenes.

Ynysmeudwy has always been noted for its childs' plates which come in a wide variety of patterns. Red Riding Hood, Women Feeding Fowls, Boy Driving Geese, A Dead Bee Maketh No Honey are all recorded in the collection of the National Museum of Wales, and Noel Riley in her excellent book on childrens' pottery records a man minding turkeys and 'This Boy I Think Looks Very Grand Driving Out His Four in Hand'.

In common with the other Welsh Potteries, Ynysmeudwy produced Mocha ware. This was made almost entirely for the pub trade and is found in the form of mugs and jugs. As ever Mocha ware is unmarked and difficult to identify accurately.

There was also some hand-decoration in the latter period at Ynysmeudwy, and much that has been found on the site is similar, but not identical, to Llanelly Persian Rose, which it predates by some years. Sponge decorated items were also made at Ynysmeudwy.

*Marks on Ynysmeudwy Pottery*

Marks on Ynysmeudwy pottery include transfer pattern marks including the name Williams or just the initials WW, and also impressed marks YNYSMEUDWY POT-TERY; YNYSMEUDWY POTTERY SWANSEA VALE and YMP.

# GAUDY WELSH

Gaudy Welsh is the term used to describe pottery and porcelain made in many parts of the British Isles and decorated in blue, red, green, and sometimes pink lustre in a variety of patterns and styles. Often it was entirely hand-painted and sometimes the blue was transferred, forming the basis of the pattern and allowing for some conformity. These patterns have developed names over the years, which they were certainly not given at the time of their manufacture, and there has been a tendency to accelerate this process, particularly on the other side of the Atlantic, to enable Gaudy Welsh to fit more readily into a collecting field.

Although Gaudy Welsh pottery is not really within the remit of this book, it does seem worthy of a passing comment in the hope of avoiding unnecessary confusion. Like copper lustre, Gaudy Welsh has always been popular in Wales and this has led to a belief that it was all made in the Principality. Some Gaudy Welsh was made by the Welsh factories, and in rather greater quantities than copper lustre which, as is mentioned elsewhere, was rarely produced in Wales. However, the vast majority of Gaudy Welsh came from Staffordshire, and very little from Wales. The confusion is further complicated by the fact that some Gaudy Welsh (and indeed sometimes all of it) is also referred to as 'Swansea Cottage'.

Both Swansea (Cambrian) and the Llanelly Potteries did produce some Gaudy Welsh. The most obvious examples from Swansea being spill vases and 'Cymro Stone China' pouch-jugs, and from Llanelly the early period Glamorgan-shaped jugs. No Gaudy Welsh or Swansea Cottage porcelain was made in Wales.

# Commemorative Pottery
## in the South Wales Factories

THE CERTAIN IDENTIFICATION OF transfer-decorated items made at the Cambrian Pottery in the early years, that is pre-1811, is notoriously difficult. There are a number of commemorative items of this period that have from time to time been attributed to Swansea but, in the absence of greater knowledge, we are restricting our list of Swansea commemoratives to items that we are certain 'beyond reasonable doubt' can be ascribed to the factory.

The first recorded Swansea commemorative is not, in fact, a transfer-decorated item but a jug, hand-decorated in cobalt blue, and commissioned by Joseph Vaughan to commemorate the victory of Admiral Rodney over the Dutch and Spanish fleets at St Eustabus in the West Indies. Joseph Vaughn's relation, Sir John Vaughn, fought with Rodney. The jug, now in the collection of the National Museum of Wales, is inscribed, *John Vaughn Melingriffey. Success to Admiral Rodney And His Majestys Navy 1781.*

In 1793, the King and Queen of France were executed in Paris. A small number of pearl-ware mugs are recorded, showing the profiles of the King and Queen of France and the King and Queen of England disguised in the pattern. The mugs are inscribed, *A New Puzzle of PORTRAITS. Striking Likeness of the King and Queen of England and the late King and Queen of France*

Nelson is known to have visited the Cambrian Pottery with the Hamiltons in 1802. Much was made of this visit and Nelson ordered pottery for himself, decorated by Thomas Pardoe, who used, for the first time, the 'Garter' star that was to become one of Pardoe's hallmarks. It seems likely that the Pottery would have commemorated some of Nelson's victories and his death in 1805, but which, if any, of the Nelson commemorative items were made at Swansea is not known. However, a large mug bearing a portrait of Nelson is certainly Swansea-painted by Thomas Pardoe.

Perhaps the finest Cambrian commemoratives of all are the Wellington jugs. These are fully marked with transfer marks, unique to them, *Dillwyn and Co Swansea* in a circle. The main transfer shows Wellington surrounded by a wreath of bay-leaves and on one side Britannia trampling a French flag and on the other side Victory. The inside rim of the jug lists the great man's battle honours. While the jugs are usually inscribed *'Wellington'*, sometimes they bear the words *'Marquis Wellington'*, a title he held briefly in 1813 before being elevated to his dukedom.

The best-known anti-Napoleon commemoratives are two variations of cartoons printed on jugs by the Cambrian Pottery in 1814. Both depict groups of good British chaps, with speech balloons emerging from their mouths, uttering all sorts of anti-Napoleon slogans. These cartoons are found in three sizes, and either in black trans-

*A Llanelly pottery jug commemorating the death of Prince Albert in 1863.*

fer on white ground with coloured enamelling or in red transfer on a 'canary' yellow ground. Many bear the signature of the engraver James Brindley.

The Glamorgan Pottery was not to be left out of this patriotic enthusiasm and produced jugs showing a seven-horned beast rising from the sea and the words *Buonoparte The Monstrous Beast.*

Two local political items were also made at about this time. The most rare of these commemorates the victory of John Owen Esq in the election for Pembroke on October 30th, 1812. The other records the victory of John Jones, of Ystrad House, in the Parliamentary election for Carmarthen in 1824.

The Great Reform Act of 1832 was the next event to stir the potters of Swansea. It seems unlikely that the Cambrian Pottery produced Reform jugs but the Glamorgan produced a variety. They were in two shapes, a round pedestal jug and the standard (though in this case rarer) Glamorgan-shaped jug. The basic print shows portraits of Althorp, Grey, Russell and Brougham in oval medallions and the words *Royal Assent to the Reform Bill 7 June 1832.* All these jugs tend to be marked with the standard Glamorgan mark of BB&I in a cartouche.

Although not strictly commemorative, it is worth mentioning the rare Glamorgan Pottery jugs depicting Daniel O'Connell and Father Matthew. These are printed in black with the words *Dan'l O'Connell Esqre* and *The very Revd Father Matthew The Two Great Regenerators of Ireland.*

The coming to the throne of Queen Victoria in 1837 was an event that was, inexplicably, not as much commemorated in ceramic terms as one might think. Thus, the items made by the Cambrian Pottery are eagerly sought after by collectors of both Welsh ceramics and commemorative items. Two different mugs were produced, both usually printed in purple. The smaller (2⅞ inches) simply shows a portrait of the Queen with the inscription QUEEN VICTORIA. The larger mug, which has an elaborate 'crested' handle, bears a similar portrait and the words *Victoria Regina Born 24th May 1819 Proclaimed 20th June 1837 Crowned 28th June 1838*. Nursery-plates bearing the same inscription were also produced. Very similar mugs were produced in Staffordshire but in these the Queen's necklace curves sinuously over the nape of her neck whereas in the Swansea version it drops straight down.

Surprisingly, the Queen's marriage to Prince Albert in 1840 was not commemorated as such. However, portrait-plates simply showing his likeness were made to the same size and pattern as the Queen's Coronation plates and may well have been produced at the time of the wedding. The portrait-plates formed part of a series which, as well as Prince Albert, also included the Revd John Wesley, the Rev John Fletcher and James Tear (or Teare – the print is found with both spellings) who was a temperance reformer.

The next commemorative to be produced was that for the royal visit to Place House at Fowey in Cornwall. From the collector's point of view, it is very interesting on a number of counts. Firstly, it was a somewhat obscure event and thus more interesting to the collector than one of national notice. Secondly, the print seems to have been used almost by default in that it is part of a series of West Country views made by the Cambrian Pottery as general souvenirs, none of the others having any commemorative connotations whatever. Thirdly, the scene, which shows the royal couple approaching Place House in an open carriage, bears the inscription *Royal Visit to Place House Fowey Sept 6th 1848*. The visit actually took place on September 8th. This rare print is found most usually on child's plates, sometimes on mugs, and very rarely on jugs.

No more commemoratives were produced in Swansea and really only one true commemorative came from the South Wales Pottery at Llanelli. This was a jug to mark the death of Prince Albert in 1863. The pattern is named simply 'Albert' and the printed factory mark W.T.H. for William Holland. The print depicts the Prince, flanked by a weeping Britannia, guarded by a very sad lion, and on the reverse side a view of Albert's greatest achievement, the Crystal Palace. These jugs are of a shape we refer to as Albert shape as they are used almost exclusively for this print.

A small number of rather crudely printed jugs are to be found from the Llanelly factory showing a named portrait of Garibaldi. Although never marked, these jugs can be identified from the individual inscriptions applied to them (a characteristic of Llanelly Pottery at that time). Dated examples show them to have been made in the 1880s but Garibaldi's celebrated visit to Great Britain (but not in fact to Wales) took place in 1864. It seems that his popularity was undiminished and that these jugs were produced at the time of his death in 1882.

# Public Collections of Welsh Pottery

THE NATIONAL MUSEUM OF WALES, Cathays Park, Cardiff.
The Sir Leslie Joseph Gallery houses the world's finest collection of Welsh ceramics.

SWANSEA MUSEUM, formerly The Royal Institution of South Wales.

THE GLYN-VIVIAN ART GALLERY, Alexandra Road, Swansea.

THE LLANELLI BOROUGH COUNCIL COLLECTION, The Mansion House (Bryncaerau), Parc Howard, Llanelli (Llanelly Pottery only).

CARMARTHEN MUSEUM, The Old Bishop's Palace, Abergwili, near Carmarthen.

# Bibliography

| | |
|---|---|
| E. Morton Nance | *The Pottery and Porcelain of Swansea and Nantgarw*, Batsford 1942 (Now available in facsimile reprint) |
| Sotheby's | *The Catalogue of the Sir Leslie Joseph Collection* |
| Dilys Jenkins | *Llanelly Pottery*, DEB Books 1968 |
| Gareth Hughes & Robert Pugh | *Llanelly Pottery*, Llanelli Borough Council 1990 |
| Helen Hallesey | *The Glamorgan Pottery at Swansea*, Gomer Press 1995 |

OTHER READING:

| | |
|---|---|
| J. & J. May | *Commemmorative Pottery 1780-1900*, Heinemann 1972 |
| Michael Gibbs & Bernard Morris | Thomas Rothwell *Views of Swansea in the 1790s* |
| John Ward | Billingsly and Pardoe, *Murray Derby 1896 (Price 3d)* |
| Noel Riley | *Gifts for Good Children*, Richard Dennis 1991 |

ARTICLES:

| | |
|---|---|
| W. Turner | Dillwyn's Etruscan Ware, *The Collector* 1907 |
| Elis Jenkins | Dillwyn's Etruscan Ware |
| Peter Price | Welsh Commemorative Pottery 1972 |
| Peter Pryce | Swansea Blue and White Pottery & S. H. Williams |
| Penelope Jones | William Weston Young 'Quaker Entrepreneur', *The Collector* 1991 |
| S. H. (Stan) Williams | Sherds from the Cambrian and Glamorgan Potteries at Swansea |
| Kildare S. Meager | The Catalogue of the Swansea and Nantgarw Pottery at the Glyn-Vivian Art Gallery Swansea 1949. |
| Derek Harper | 'Ynysmeudwy Pottery' in Vol. III of *Minerva* (The Transactions of the Royal Institution of South Wales). |

The Catalogue of the Special Loan Exhibition at the Glyn Vivian Art Gallery 1914
English Ceramic Circle Transactions 1967   Swansea Pottery by Grant Davidson
English Ceramic Circle Transactions 1968   Thomas Rothwell by Norman Stretton

# Chronological list of important events in the South Wales potteries

| | |
|---|---|
| 1764 | Commencement of Cambrian Pottery |
| 1768 | First recorded dated item |
| 1786 | Arrival of George Haynes |
| 1790 | Rothwell already in Swansea |
| 1792 | Rothwell leaves Swansea |
| 1795 | Thomas Pardoe arrives in Swansea |
| 1802 | Dillwyn purchases Cambrian |
| 1802 | Nelson's visit |
| 1803 | William Weston Young commences work at Cambrian |
| 1806 | W. W. Young leaves Cambrian |
| 1809 | Thomas Pardoe leaves Swansea |
| 1810 | George Haynes leaves Cambrian |
| 1811 | L. W. Dillwyn partnership with Bevingtons |
| 1814 | Commencement of Glamorgan Pottery |
| 1814 | (Oct.) Commencement of porcelain manufacture at Swansea |
| 1817 | Bevington & Co. |
| 1824 | Return of L. W. Dillwyn |
| 1831 | L. Ll. Dillwyn takes over the Cambrian Pottery |
| 1839 | Dillwyn buys Glamorgan Pottery |
| 1840 | South Wales Pottery commences |
| 1842 | Dyfatty St. Pottery opens |
| 1850 | Cambrian taken over by Evans & Glasson |
| 1852/56 | Callands Pottery, Landore |
| 1855 | Chambers leaves Llanelli |
| 1855 | Lewis Weston Dillwyn died |
| 1855/58 | Llanelly Coombs & Holland period |
| 1856 | Ynysmeudwy Pottery opens |
| 1858/75 | Llanelly W. T. Holland period |
| 1870 | Ynysmeudwy Pottery closes |
| 1870 | Cambrian Pottery closes |
| 1875 | Llanelly closes |
| 1878 | Llanelly re-opened. Guest & Dewsberry period |
| 1892 | Dyfatty Street Pottery closes |
| 1908 | Arrival of Samuel Shufflebotham at Llanelly |
| 1922 | Llanelly Pottery closes |

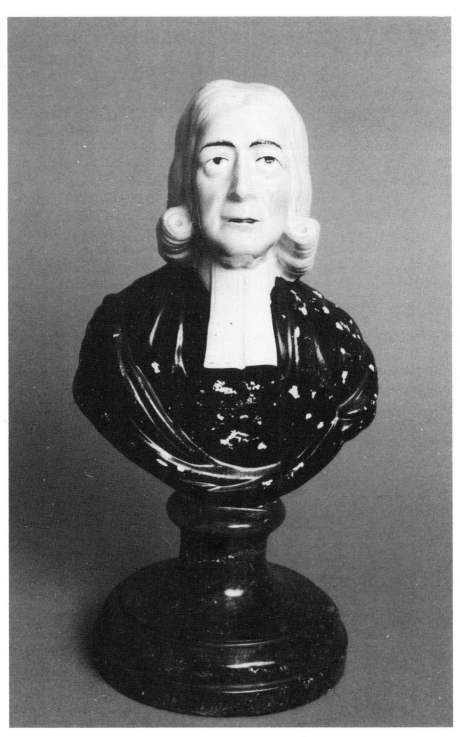

*A very rare bust of John Wesley made at the South Wales Pottery, Llanelly, c.1840,*
*marked William Chambers Jnr South Wales Pottery.*
*(Photograph: Andrew Dando).*